THE PROFITABLE CONTRACTOR

How to Attract Better Clients, Make More Money, and Create the Contracting Business You Really Want

THE PROFITABLE CONTRACTOR

How to Attract Better Clients, Make More Money, and Create the Contracting Business You Really Want

STEVE DALE

Niche Pressworks

THE PROFITABLE CONTRACTOR

Copyright © 2021 by Steve Dale

All rights reserved. No part of this book may be used or reproduced in any manner whatsoever without prior written consent of the author, except as provided by the United States of America copyright law. For permission to reprint portions of this content, or for bulk purchases, contact the author at Steve@24onCenter.com

The views expressed herein are solely those of the author and do not necessarily reflect the views of the publisher.

The names and identifying details of some individuals mentioned throughout the book have been changed to protect their privacy.

Published by Niche Pressworks: http://NichePressworks.com
Indianapolis, IN

ISBN: 978-1-952654-17-6 Paperback
      978-1-952654-18-3 eBook

DEDICATION

To my wife Andrea, who has lovingly stuck by my side through both the good and tough times in my contracting career.

To my three kids—Isaiah, Iyla, and Ezra—being your dad has made me view life in a new and meaningful way. We have many years left to enjoy this life, and I pray we make each day count!

To each and every one of YOU. The remodel contracting field is tough, especially when it feels like you are doing it all alone. This book will guide you to making the changes necessary to create the career you want.

CONTENTS

Introduction: The Day I Woke Up to My Reality 1
    When I Started to See the Light 2

Chapter 1: Build Your Life Back! 5
    My "Aha" Moment 5
    A 41% Markup 6
    Reasons to Stay in the Home Remodeling Business 8
    How You Run Your Business 10
    Which Path Do You Want? 11
    Are You Listening? 12

Chapter 2: The ONE Thing You Need to Know 15
    Myth #1: A referral client is a better client 18
    Myth #2: You have to bend over backwards to please a client 19
    Myth #3: You must work for past clients 19
    Myth #4: Volume is everything! 20
    Myth #5: You must entertain all prospects 20
    Myth #6: You will get ahead by working more hours 20
    Myth #7: I MADE it! This new job will take me to the next level 21
    Give Up the Myths 21

Chapter 3: What's Holding You Back? 23
    Your Mindset 23

    You Arrogant Bastard 24
  Your Numbers 25
  Avoiding a Crash. 25
  You Need to Charge More 26
  Crabs In a Bucket 27

Chapter 4: Small Changes, Big Impact 29
  Lessons from a Dishwasher 29
  Make Sure to Use the Right Numbers 30
    Markup 31
    Profit Margin 31
    Proposal Fees 32
  Quick Business Wins 35
  Stop Fooling Yourself 36

Chapter 5: The Right Clients Are the Key 37
  The Right Clients 38
  Red Flags 39
  Time-Wasters. 39
  Right Clients Improve Your Life 42
  Keys to Success 43
  Right Clients = Right Revenue 43
  Client Review Checklist 44
  Right Clients Are The Golden Ticket 45

Chapter 6: How to Get Top Clients: Basic 47
  Know Your Brand 49
  Build Value. 49
  Under Promise and Over Deliver 50
  Understand Marketing 51
    Get Testimonials. 51
    Ask for Client Referrals 52
  Stick with the New Process 52

Chapter 7: How to Price Your Services: Next Level 53
  What Is Your Time Worth? 53

A Former Idaho Tile "Contractor" 54
Running Your Business 55
Fair Pricing 56
Race to the Bottom? 57
Differentiate Yourself 58
    What Are Your BIGGEST Strengths? 58
    How Do You Add Value? 59
Immutable Laws 59
Price Should Match Your Value 60
Run PROFITABLE Jobs 61

Chapter 8: Kick-Start Your Business ... Now 63
    Don't Be Afraid to Say "No" 64
    Final Question 65

Chapter 9: You've Got This! 67
    Step One: Commit to Change 68
    Step Two: Work with Top Clients 68
    Step Three: Have Patience 68
    Step Four: Enjoy What's Next 69

Thank You 71

Want My Help? 73

About Steve Dale 75

INTRODUCTION

THE DAY I WOKE UP TO MY REALITY

I'm lying in bed on a Saturday morning. My wife is already up with the kids, and I can hear them laughing over the sound of the Saturday morning cartoons.

Last night, I had worked until eight and then ended up watching YouTube videos about how to run a successful construction business. I was running behind on the current job and had promised the client that I'd go back today to finish things up—another Saturday working.

As I started to roll out of bed, resentful that I was missing a day with my kids, it flashed before me—I'm not working for people I particularly like or respect, and yet, I keep showing up for them. My clients treat me like I'm a pack animal, a burro they can just whack on the butt as they throw another load on my back.

Why am I spending all my time with these people and not with my family? Something is wrong with this picture. This is not why I worked so hard to become skilled at construction or why I wanted to run my own business or why I went even further and earned a business degree.

Walking upstairs, I was thinking of the times I had missed my son's soccer games and my wife's birthdays. These thoughts were in my mind just as the sun glinted on the table, and it was like a lightbulb turned on—I needed to make a change. I couldn't build or improve my business doing what I had been doing (or with YouTube videos). What I was doing was not working. Period.

I couldn't go on doing this by myself. I needed a unique, new perspective to address the issues in my business. YouTube videos were coping mechanisms. They gave me the impression that I was moving forward and making progress when I was really just spinning my wheels. The videos covered surface issues and never went into detail.

They never addressed the inner game, the things no one talks about when running a construction business.

When I Started to See the Light

Once the idea of change got in my head, I was committed. I didn't want to waste another Saturday away from my wife and kids working for someone I didn't particularly respect who treated my team poorly.

The personal cost was way too high. I had:

- Missed my son's soccer games
- Missed my wife's birthday (and didn't plan her a party)
- Missed family vacation time
- Cut hiking and hunting trips short
- Sacrificed my health by not making time to exercise
- Fallen behind on household projects
- Worked too many hours to be thoughtful to my wife—buying her gifts and surprising her
- Missed out on my kids' school events

All along, I had been thinking, "This is what running a business is like. I know what I'm doing." But I didn't. I'd been doing all the things I know how to do, and it wasn't working. To get where I wanted to be with my business and my life, I needed something to change.

At the time, I didn't fully understand it, but something big shifted in me that morning. When I look back on it today, I see that I realized what I had been avoiding: I was never going to be able to do this by myself.

I had my business degree, tried my best, did everything I could think of, and even prayed, but it wasn't working. I needed another perspective. And that's why two days later, I talked to a business coach.

Paying someone for advice was not something I'd ever considered. Would it really be possible for a business coach to help me figure out how to solve my dilemma? Could I improve my business and get more time with my wife and children?

In our first conversation, the business coach got my attention. He said, "Look, you're the common denominator! All these clients, they're different people. It's a different person every time. But the same thing keeps happening. You're the common denominator. What we need to do is work on you." It was the hardest thing to hear, and I did not want to believe it. I still wanted to think I knew everything I needed to run a profitable contracting business, but I needed to make a change, and boy, did this one pay off.

Usually, I run higher costs by my wife before committing, but this time I didn't. I guess I felt like it would be easier to ask for forgiveness than permission, and I was at the end of my rope. At first, I admit, my wife was upset because she saw it as an expense. She was calculating the hourly cost of the coaching to which I had just committed myself.

After a few sessions, we both started to realize that it wasn't an expense. It was an investment. The business coach helped me think outside of the box I'd built. He helped me see things in new ways, and this is where my journey to a better business began.

> AFTER A FEW SESSIONS, WE BOTH STARTED TO REALIZE THAT IT WASN'T AN EXPENSE. IT WAS AN INVESTMENT.

Keep in mind: On paper, it looked like I had a successful business. I normally had a waiting list. I was booked out for months, and people were waiting for me to start their projects. Most contractors would say these things are the keys to success. Still, I was unhappy and overworked. I knew something had to change. I was maxed out with clients, and there are only so many hours in the day. I had no more to give and definitely no room to grow my business.

Working with my business coach helped me identify exactly what I wanted: to earn more income while working fewer hours. We all want that, right? But I worked with my business coach to make changes that would make it happen. After a few months, I was making it home at a decent hour almost every night and wasn't working weekends. Over time, I continued to discover all kinds of amazing things as my business became more profitable.

It had seemed impossible to me, but here I was, becoming the guy I wanted to be again: happy and friendly with time for his kids, present in his daily life, and someone who makes his wife feel appreciated. This is what I want for you too. This book is about amplifying not just your business but your life. Yes, it is possible.

Having a business coach changed everything. With my success, I realized I needed to share what I'd learned. I know what it's like to run a contracting business. This book is meant to help turn your business into something that supports your family and life, rather than a millstone around your neck. I suspect that's why you're still reading this, and I know you can do it. If I could do it, you can. You will be so happy you did.

My hope is that you are reading this book because you want to approach your business with an entrepreneurial spirit. The usual way you're doing business isn't working. In fact, it might be set up for failure because nobody helped you look at how to run your business well. If you're like I was, you might be listening to your buddy about his business ideas. And what makes his ideas the ones that you should listen to? Even if his business seems better than yours from the outside, chances are it isn't. Just like I did, you've probably been trying hard to figure this out on your own, with little or no success. It's not your fault, and it isn't your buddy's fault either. Nobody has taught you correctly.

Don't let pride get in the way. If you are sick and tired of the exhausting hours and clients taking advantage of you, let me tell you, there is a better way. Listen to my story and open yourself up to the possibility of implementing some new ideas. This book can show you how to start turning things around to create the contracting business of your dreams.

In the following pages, you'll read how my One-Year Rescue Plan can help lead you down a path to become *The Profitable Contractor* you want to be and create a new and better life for you, your family, and your employees.

Create a new, better life. I'm excited for you. It's going to be amazing.

CHAPTER 1

BUILD YOUR LIFE BACK!

The reality is that your business model is screwing you. You just can't see it yet. I know this because I'm a contractor. Just like you, I was running a business that was running me into the ground. After years of always feeling behind, I was able to turn things around, and I'm going to show how you can do it too.

I may not know the specific details of your business, and I can't claim that my strategy will have the same results for you, but I am going to show you what worked amazingly well for me. It's my hope that you will be able to take this information and use it to get on the right track so you can achieve the results you want.

If you're looking for a quick fix that will turn things around overnight, this book isn't it. We're going to make changes that will create a better business for the long run. So, if you understand that self-awareness will help you win the game and are willing to roll up your sleeves and do some hard work, then this is the book for you.

As you're reading, I may ask you to pause and complete a task. Take a minute, and do it! If you're serious about creating a better future for your business and your family, doing the work is the only thing that will get you there.

So, let's get started!

My "Aha" Moment

In the early spring of 2017, I realized that even though I had a business degree, for some reason, I was not applying it. I was running a contracting business but had settled into just adopting the standards that other contractors were using for their businesses, believing that was just how things were done.

Until one day, I woke up and realized that I'd created a business I did not want ... and it wasn't what my family wanted either. I was living from job to job, working seven days a week, and every year was exactly the same as the last one. My business degree had taught me finance and strategy but had not prepared me to be an entrepreneur.

Hiring a business coach was the **single best thing I did** to move my business in the right direction. Finding the right business coach for you is essential. They don't all have the exact tools and know-how to help you improve your contracting business. I think this is the hang-up for many contractors out there—they know people who have paid for fancy consultants, but the "fixes" they suggest don't fully translate to our business.

You might think you are not ready for a change right now. Or maybe you think that your business is too set to switch things up. But believe me, it's not too soon—or too late.

A 41% Markup

You read that right. Forty-one percent. That's the minimum markup I now need in order to take a job. This percentage ensures a job is profitable while still being able to keep the doors open. But a 41% markup wasn't always the case.

I knew my education, experience, and knowledge were worth more than I was earning. But I was lucky if I could get a 20% markup on a job. This was not because I didn't want to sell the job for more. Every other contractor I knew was having a difficult time getting much above a 15% markup. I was stuck at 20% because I just figured there was no way I could ask for more than that.

Luckily, my business coach helped me see the numbers from a different perspective so I could make some major adjustments. The first step was a mental shift. I had to realize and accept that my markup costs were going to be more than everyone around me. Then, I had to recognize that this healthy markup was not selfish. It was the exact opposite. In order for my business to succeed, my family's financial needs had to be met. My markup costs needed to cover expenses so that, at the end of the day, there was a net profit remaining.

Basically, you have to mark up your jobs. This is my number. What is yours? Forty-one percent allows me to generate the revenue needed to make a profit. I'm getting paid for more than just line items and time. I'm getting paid for the value I provide, which allows me to be selective about the clients I work for. I'm no longer a victim of my business.

Getting to this point meant I had to think about my business on my own terms, starting with markups. Some contractors I knew were not even charging a markup on their materials because they felt it was unfair to the customer. Or, they thought it was highway robbery to mark up their subcontractors more than 10 to 15%. Not a great way to structure a profitable business. Why would a contractor even think that? There are no rules that say that anywhere. The only robbery was from their own bank account and time spent with family.

Of course, this had been my own thinking for many years. It seemed to be the going rate, so I thought that cost plus 10 to 15% was "fair" to a client. But it sure wasn't fair to me. The crazy thing is that I knew it was wrong, but I kept doing it because I did not know what else to do.

If this sounds familiar, now you know that you are not alone. But also know that if you continue to follow this model, like me, you will work your tail off and struggle just to survive and support your family. And you probably won't ever have many extra funds (or time) to do fun things with them.

I kept searching for answers outside my business. But when I talked to that coach, the tough questions he asked got me thinking. And that was when I had my light-bulb moment.

Ultimately, I was responsible for the pain and suffering that I was inflicting on myself and my family. I was stressed out all the time. There was huge financial friction with my wife that would often lead to arguments. And I frequently had a very short fuse with my kids—sometimes over nothing, just for playing the way kids do. It was a hard realization. This was not the husband and father I wanted to be.

The coach made it clear that there was lots of work to do. And I will tell you the same thing. Simply adding a healthy markup factor doesn't necessarily mean you are going to be profitable. It just means you are on your way to understanding your numbers a little better. But this can be a quick win. It was most definitely mine! And it helps you start to see that improvement is possible.

So, after my aha moment, I went all in. I never looked back and was not offended if a client didn't understand my price. There was no more "sharpening the pencil" on my numbers—no more shaving a bit off here and there to make the client happy. I understood that this is what it took to become profitable.

I'm still a little embarrassed to think that someone with my background and experience thought it was okay to put in so many hours—and sacrifice so much family time—and still barely stay afloat. But now, with my better understanding of how the contracting world works, I'm energized by the unlimited possibilities in our industry to be successful. When you begin to make changes to create a successful, profitable business, that translates to success for you and your family.

Plan your future and start today. When you take your next job, be firm. Stick to your guns and remember that this is the amount you have to get to make the job work. If they turn you down, move on, and let the next guy struggle with it. (Actually, you may eventually want to help him out as well, but you need to take care of yourself first.) Taking this initial step starts you on the path to success and gives you more freedom to enjoy your life.

Reasons to Stay in the Home Remodeling Business

Some of you might be thinking that it would be easier to just find a different line of work rather than completely redesigning your business. But there are many reasons why you don't need to do that, including those listed below.

1. **The opportunity is HUGE!** For starters, Baby Boomers are one of the largest segments of the population, and they've got money to invest in their homes. Additionally, more young families are opting to stay put in better neighborhoods to raise their kids, choosing to make improvements to existing homes rather than move. The average mid- to high-level homeowner remodels

every ten to fifteen years. Understand who your top clients are and look for the neighborhoods where they live.

2. **You've already got the tools and the skills.** Taking your business to the next level is about being business savvy. But it doesn't take a big capital investment. You're already good at this. You just need some tools to shift your focus on how to make it more profitable.
3. **You can get paid in advance!** In my business, we get paid for the job before we start.
4. **HGTV.** Let's face it. As contractors, we generally hate starry-eyed HGTV fans. But the reality is that the shows on this network (and those like it) are driving a massive amount of business our way! We want our prospects watching HGTV, as long as we can conquer the top challenge in our business: setting realistic expectations. Once you've got that down, you become the visionary of their next makeover.
5. **You have FULL CONTROL.** One of my wife's favorite movies is *Pretty Woman*. Usually, I tune the movie out while watching with her, but there is one line that always gets my attention. Julia Roberts says, "I say who, and I say when!" That's what you want (and can have) when you're not just taking any job to make the next buck. When you're the boss, you can schedule your jobs around your family plans. I used to think this was impossible, but once I cracked this code, my family and I schedule vacations and keep them. We decide when we want to go and put it on the calendar. My clients are important, but my family, the reason I run my business, is more important.
6. **#KEEPCRAFTALIVE.** The truth is, you and I are a rare breed. There aren't enough of us. And there's very little competition—especially when we're GOOD. The truth is that the older generation is retiring, and not enough of the younger generation is getting into the trades. The opportunity is there, and you want to be part of the movement!

<u>In fact,</u> the U.S. Bureau of Labor Statistics projects the annual average job openings in the trades industry through 2028 will exceed 1.2 million jobs. And each occupation in the trades category is either growing at a *faster than average* or much *faster than average* rate.[1]

---

[1] "Employment Projections Home Page," U.S. Bureau of Labor Statistics, https://www.bls.gov/emp/.

How You Run Your Business

When managing your own business, there are three general paths you can take:

You can keep doing what you've always done.

If you're satisfied with your situation, great. If not, doing what you've always done means accepting where you are and ignoring your family and money problems. If you do this, things will be exactly the same this time next year. GUARANTEED. Your problems will not magically go away if you don't make any changes.

You can DIY your own clean-up.

I tried this for many years. I started following a lot of people on social media, watched countless YouTube videos, and tried a bunch of different fixes. Of course, this is the equivalent of a homeowner watching DIY videos online to try to repair something on their own. (You've probably gotten some of those desperate calls when they realize they're in over their head.) They failed because they didn't know what they were doing—watching a video is no substitute for actual know-how.

This was my experience trying to DIY my business at first. Lots of attempts at improving things, but none were successful because I didn't understand how all the pieces fit together. And as I discovered, you can only learn so much by watching YouTube videos or asking other contractors what they're doing.

If you're still at a point in your business where you have more time than money, then yes, you can start to clean up your business yourself and make some progress. This book will help you get started.

You can hire a pro to help you improve faster.

Commit to yourself and your business by investing in expert coaching to systematically remodel your business. One of my favorite business quotes is, "Take the fastest path to the results you want." Hiring a coach transformed my business and my life and turned my struggling business into a profitable one … and it ignited a passion in me to get certified as a coach so I could help others.

You need someone with experience who can show you exactly what to do, where, and when. The order matters. The process matters. Having an expert helping you every step of the way is the fastest path (and it will save you a heck of a lot of headaches in wasted time and money). A coach can also help you make a lot of money faster.

Which Path Do You Want?

The choice is clear. Follow a proven process with methodologies that have helped many business owners understand their worth—and fall back in love with their business. With these changes, their personal relationships and health improved as well.

I understand that the decision to make a change in your business can create some fear and anxiety. These are normal feelings. And I am not telling you that you cannot figure it out on your own. I am saying it is very difficult to do when you are running your business—focusing on your current jobs/clients/employees, fielding phone calls, looking at new prospective jobs, working on estimates and proposals, delivering the proposals, invoicing, collecting payments on jobs, etc. When in the heck do you actually have the EXTRA time to invest in thinking about and making DIY micro changes to your business processes?

You want RESULTS, so you need to be honest with yourself. Do you have that much extra time and energy? If not, it is likely that at this time next year, you will be right where you are now—doing

> YOU WANT RESULTS, SO YOU NEED TO BE HONEST WITH YOURSELF.

what you're currently doing. Your family and financial situation will be the same. You will be working for the same exact clients you currently are.

Let's take another look in the future. Years down the road, do you want to be that crabby sixty-year-old contractor guy, hunched back, walking with a limp from bad hips, or limited arm movement from shoulder surgeries—all things that stemmed from working 24/7 and not taking care of yourself?

We all know those guys. Often, they're also divorced. And sometimes not just once, but two or three times. Their kids are barely in touch because their dad was never there for them.

All these things can result from letting your business consume you. Are you on track to be that guy? Just because you are so strong-willed and don't think you need anyone else's help? Do you want to risk ending up lonely, depressed, and still working as hard as ever because your income has always been week to week, job to job, and you're scrambling to pay your taxes every year?

OR, do you want to be this guy:

You are sixty years old, and because you have been taking care of yourself, positivity exudes from you. You've made time in your life for exercise and healthy eating, so you still feel youthful. You and your wife are planning your next wedding anniversary trip, and you just got back from a resort vacation in Hawaii.

As you arrive home, you excitedly begin preparing for your two kids and six grandchildren to come home for an extended Thanksgiving holiday. You have a solid relationship with your kids. They respect you and are willing to ask for your advice. And they themselves are making very wise decisions as young adults because as they were growing up, they watched you make smart choices and run a successful business.

Money isn't an issue, and this allows you to donate to great causes and experience things in life. You realize that these things are only possible because of the decisions you made when you were in your thirties that changed the direction of your contracting business.

Are You Listening?

I see contractors all the time who are in the trap from the first example. They have so much pride and think they can figure it out on their own. The longer they let it go, the harder it is to think about making changes (old dogs think they can't learn new tricks).

But I know there is a way out of this mess and into the life you and your family are craving. And I understand that it is difficult to see the label on the jar when we are stuck inside it. I was there.

Our brains can only handle so much. And when you are consumed by running a business, it's easier to keep making bad decisions and try to put out the fires later. A wonderful mentor of mine reminds me of this quite often, and there's so much truth to it.

I still have a business coach. All successful coaches have coaches or someone who creates tremendous value in their lives and businesses. There are things in my business that I still need help with. So do not think that seeking out help means you are a failure. It means the exact opposite. You are wise and want to get to the next level.

How do you want to be judged by your family ten years down the road? What kind of husband and father do you want them to remember? You can be the change. You can be the HERO in their life. Your vision and purpose in life are not being fulfilled, are they?

Following a proven process like the One-Year Rescue Plan can help you relieve stress, gain confidence, and allow you to start realizing that you do have what it takes to succeed at this.

CHAPTER 2

THE ONE THING YOU NEED TO KNOW

So, let's talk about what business really is. You've probably been thinking you're a business owner. But in my experience, most contractors are job owners, and the business owns them—24/7.

If you can't walk away from your business for a week or a month and still get paid, you have a job. And there's a big difference between having a job and owning a business.

Your Business Model Is Screwing You

It's not the industry or the clients that are the problem. It's your business model. You do not know how to run your business profitably … yet. It is not your fault, but it is your problem. You were likely always told to focus on your craft. Meaning, if you are good at what you do, you'll make money—and the harder you work, the more you will make.

> IT IS NOT YOUR FAULT, BUT IT IS YOUR PROBLEM.

The truth is, that is a road to disaster. And it can lead to a slow, painful death. You don't want to be that old guy with a busted up body, divorced, bad relationships with your kids, limited finances, and no opportunities to experience and explore life. You have put in the time and effort and should be rewarded for all your hard work.

Fixing the way you think about and run your business is the key to creating the business you really want.

Your inner self might be telling you this is not possible. It might be telling you to quit. You might think, "You don't understand. My clients expect me to be available all the time." Or, "Well, maybe that worked for you and another guy or gal, but it won't work for my business."

I would counter these objections with a few things learned over the years. First, catering to unreasonably demanding clients is not sustainable. Second, you only assume that changing things in your business isn't possible because no one has shown you exactly how to take the next steps.

This is your business. You're the owner. You're responsible for its future and what you want for you, your family, your employees, and maybe even future generations.

Make a bold move. Commit to making a change and take the first step now.

Your Biggest Pain

STOP. Write down the names of three clients you would love to FIRE and never have back in your life again. Getting rid of clients like this will have a huge impact on your contracting business. I'll cover this in more detail later in the book.

1) _____
2) _____
3) _____

You Have to Fix the Business

You want to work smarter, not harder. You want to attract the right clients who come to you and pay you what you are worth. I bet that the three clients you identified above are not doing this.

Fixing your business starts with CLARITY in a few key areas:

VISION: What is the business you really want? For many years, I thought my company's vision was to make it to the end of the week, then the end of the month, and hopefully, complete all the jobs in that year. I also hoped that I could have a couple of Saturdays with my family, be home from work by 6:00 pm on a regular basis, and maybe, take a vacation. But really, that is not a VISION at all. That's just SURVIVAL.

What my coach helped me realize is that your vision shouldn't just be getting by. It should reflect what you actually want your life and business to be. You need to be extremely clear about what you want and make it as tangible as possible.

IDEAL CLIENT: Who do you want to work with? Shouldn't it be someone who respects you and is happy to pay your fee? Shouldn't you enjoy working for this client? While high revenue jobs may seem more profitable, they do not necessarily mean a client is ideal for your business and vision. They, too, can be a real pain in the ass.

MESSAGE: What do you want people to think of you and your brand? Once you determine that, you need to create strong marketing that communicates this with a clear message. How can you create emotion with your message so that it will resonate with your ideal client? Who are you attracting with your current message?

VALUE: How do you ensure you're paid what you're worth? You are the expert. You're a professional and have gained knowledge that the prospects need. They don't set the price. You do. Your responsibility is to know how to price a job based on the skills, labor, and materials it will take to do it well. Yes, the market price needs to be considered, but that does not mean you can only charge what everyone else does. The market does not dictate your business model or survival.

DELIVERY PROCESS: How do you deliver on what you promised and do it with excellence? When you have solid business systems in place, your ability to do a job well is supported at every stage of the process—marketing, quoting, doing the job, and even completing paperwork.

Start with Better Clients

I've given you examples of how simple things can make a valuable difference. There are lots of these details inside your business, too. Simple tweaks and slight changes to the way you do things can make a four- or five-figure difference in your profits.

But don't make the mistake of thinking all you have to do is start charging more. Remember, markup does not equal profit. You are most likely marking up projects now yet still losing money. Just charging more money and keeping the same business practices won't change your business or your life.

The single biggest change you need to make is choosing to work with only top or ideal clients. These are the clients who will give you a thriving and PROFITABLE business. Once you have those top clients, they will value your time and have no problem paying you what you're worth. And once you are getting paid for the exceptional value you provide, your profits will improve. And you will enjoy serving these clients.

Top clients expect a professional experience. And it all starts with first impressions—the first visit, the proposal, communication, etc. So those processes need to be in tip-top shape to build the client list you want (and need). Later in the book, we'll talk about setting up systems.

Before we discuss the ideal customer and how to identify them, let's talk about a few myths you may have about clients.

Common Myths

The following client situations are fact, not fiction. I have experienced all of these, and you probably have as well.

Myth #1: A referral client is a better client.

I understand that you are a person of integrity, someone with strong values and a people pleaser, right? Although you may feel obligated to take on a client and their project, let's take a deeper look. A client passes your name along to a friend of a friend. This creates a sense of pride and excitement. It's a great feeling, isn't it?

Truth: Did you really like working for the client that referred you? Or did they complain about every detail and make you bend over backward for them? Maybe you incurred more job expenses than expected or stayed late and worked weekends—all to make sure you left the client happy. Of course, they are going to refer you. Why wouldn't they? You gave them exceptional craftsmanship, never left their side, and did it all for an extraordinary price. But do you really want to have another job like that? You can be sure that the friend they referred will expect the exact same thing.

Referral clients are some of the best clients you can have for your business. But you need to make sure they meet the qualifications for what you consider a desirable client. You probably should only plan to accept referrals from your ideal clients. Once you establish who your top clients are and understand your sweet spot, you will look forward to job referrals that come from them. Until then, tread lightly, my friend.

Myth #2: You have to bend over backwards to please a client.

How in the hell can they think that's even reasonable?! What are they thinking? Are they confused ... or insane? The client is not the king of your business. These difficult clients might want you to look at their project when "they" are free and off of work. That means evenings or weekends when you are supposed to be having family time. Or if something unexpected comes up during a job, they're likely to expect you to make changes for free.

Truth: These clients are never (I mean NEVER) happy with what you do. I spent many years bending over backwards for clients. In the end, it always turned out the same—the projects end up costing you more and requiring many more resources than you can afford if you want any profit. Not to mention all of the stress this type of client puts you through. I mentioned being a people pleaser, and this might be part of your personality (it is definitely part of mine). Know that about yourself, and don't allow other people to change your plan—it's not going to help you reach your business potential. You have to leverage your time and set boundaries with your clients.

Myth #3: You must work for past clients.

Every time they call you, it's a new, different project. They LOVE your work and you as well. The previous jobs weren't the best, but at least you know what you're getting into, right?

Truth: The truth is that they always want extras and think you should include them since they are "giving you all this work." And since you've given them this kind of service with past projects, of course, they expect it again. You might be tempted to try to justify it—you understand you may not make as much as you would like, but you're positive you will make it up on the next job with them, or even on your next client's project. Don't fall for it.

Once you start really looking at your business, you will understand who the top clients are. Some of your past clients are going to make the cut, but I am 100% certain you have clients you will never need to work for again.

Myth #4: Volume is everything!

I know, I know, you've got lots of work—you're booking jobs four to six months out. You feel like you could maybe even handle a few more customers. More business means more revenue, right? And you don't want to risk tarnishing your reputation by turning people away.

Truth: The only way to win on volume is to be priced the cheapest. If you keep lowering your prices to compete with your competition, you'll be out of business in five years, if not sooner! Walmart can compete with volume. The Walmart business model won't work for you.

Myth #5: You must entertain all prospects.

The phone won't stop ringing, and the requests keep coming in. You look at your upcoming estimates/bids and fit in every opportunity because more jobs mean more money. All clients are alike—a customer is a customer, right?

Truth: This myth is similar to the myth about volume. You just can't take every meeting. When you serve everyone, you serve nobody. There already isn't enough of you to go around, and every phone call or visit is taking your time and skills away from current jobs. You have to prioritize. So ask yourself if this a job you want. Or, more importantly, does the prospect seem to be a good fit for your business? Once you have a more defined system to prequalify prospects, it will be easier to screen out the jobs and clients that are not in your best interest.

Myth #6: You will get ahead by working more hours.

Business success is measured by how busy I am. Everyone is eager to work with my business, so if I have to work longer hours, at least it's going to pay off. And family and friends give me high fives for working long days and weekends.

Truth: Working longer hours does not lead to success. It is not sustainable and can lead to burnout, mistakes, and accidents.

Myth #7: I MADE it! This new job will take me to the next level.

You're excited and proud and willing to do anything and everything to make this big opportunity work. All your hard work and long hours are finally paying off. This is a project you have been waiting for—it could be your big break. You have made it to the next level and might even be able to hire more team members. If this one goes well, then maybe more of these big jobs will be headed your way.

Truth: The reality is that one big job isn't going to fix your business. You are not being truthful with yourself. Sure, getting a nice big contract is what we all want, and it CAN help your business tremendously. But not if the foundations of your business haven't been fixed. Just like building a house, you need to start with the foundation—the most important part of the project. If it's not solid, sooner or later, it's going to catch up with you.

Give Up the Myths

If any of the myths above sound familiar to you, it's likely you are attracting the wrong clients. I bought into these same client myths too—the client is always right; repeat clients are the best; you just need more jobs; referrals are always great; etc. The problem is, this is total BS. And once you start going down this path, you must take intentional steps to turn things around.

I understand that it may seem like these myths are the norm. Many of your contracting buddies are doing the exact same thing, working countless hours every day of the week. You're all busting your butts, and you deserve to reap more financial rewards for your efforts. But I'm here to tell you. **There is a better way.**

CHAPTER 3

WHAT'S HOLDING YOU BACK?

When Stacey, a friend, mentor, and coach of mine, is learning something new, she always says, "I've never been better at it than I am now, and I'm improving every time I try."

I really like this thinking. Sure, it can be scary to try something new and different. It's a natural reaction to the unknown, but improving a situation usually requires change. We have to put our fears away, address any legitimate objections, and understand that we will be challenged along the way. Achieving the goal will be worth it.

Your Mindset

If you want change, you have to make it happen. The key is adjusting your mindset. It probably won't be perfect at first, and it does not have to be. You are trying something new, so it will seem unfamiliar and take some practice.

It might be difficult at first, and you may think you're not getting it quite right. That's where Stacey's refrain kicks in—you'll improve every time you try.

You need to understand going in that there will be challenges along the way. There may be voices chirping in your ear, telling you it's a bad idea or that it's not possible.

Skepticism is understandable. Fear is a natural reaction to the unknown. It's possible you won't even know anyone else in the business who is changing the way they do things. If they're making it, why should you take the risk? That's the first thing you need to change. What's really holding you back is yourself and your mindset. You have to believe that you can do it.

You don't have to do it alone. If you follow a proven process that has helped hundreds of businesses, it's likely to help yours. On the other hand, not trying guarantees you'll fail. If you commit to improving a little bit each day, you'll start to see results.

You Arrogant Bastard

You may be thinking that about me and wondering, "If this is so great, why isn't everyone doing it? All of the contractors I know are at cost plus 10% to 15% markup, and they seem to be getting plenty of work."

First of all, someone saying they're succeeding doesn't mean they are. You don't know if their business is even profiting or how much debt they might be in. What they drive or where they live doesn't tell you this either. People can portray themselves as they want others to see them. Don't assume that they're successful just because it seems that way to you.

Let's address some common objections and concerns, and talk about a truth for many contractors: **They don't want to learn the numbers.**

> THEY DON'T WANT TO LEARN THE NUMBERS.

So which numbers do you really need to know? Well, the short answer is all of them. If you're the owner, you should be aware of every financial detail related to your business.

Do you know exactly what your business expenses are—and which kind they are? (Did you even know that there are more than one kind?)

Direct costs can easily be traced directly to the production of a good or service. Examples would be materials (finishes, fixtures, etc.), salaries, and wages.

Indirect costs cannot be traced directly to the production of a good or service. Examples would be administrative costs, marketing, etc. Indirect costs need to be allocated to the product or service you provide your customers.

Every job needs to factor in these costs. Yet so many contractors don't keep track of them, much less factor them into proposals.

Too many contractors use the **"arbitrary number"** method. Let me tell you—this is NOT a method. By definition, arbitrary means something random and not based on reason or a system.

But so many contractors still rely on this. The only reasoning is that this is familiar—the way they've always done things. Or maybe they're picking numbers based on what the contractor down the street charges. Neither of these will result in sound business decisions.

You have the desire and the will to run a profitable business. You love your work and cannot think of doing anything else. You are better at your craft than most of those other guys. You should be getting paid what you're worth.

Your Numbers

You need to get comfortable with the facts and figures—your numbers—so you can get paid based on your value and expertise. Have you ever sat down to calculate what you need to be profitable? Think about these questions:

How much profit do you want to make per job?
What are all of the wages for each job?
What are your direct expenses?
What are your indirect expenses?
How much do you, the owner, want to make on the job besides profit?
What lifestyle are you trying to support?

Avoiding a Crash

Holy $%#@! That's a mountain!

My friend Joe Levitch once told me a story about the time he almost crashed into a mountain. Joe is a general contractor in Boise, Idaho. He owns Levco Builders and is a master certified remodeler. One pitch-black night while working as a flight paramedic for Life Flight, he and his pilot were in a helicopter surrounded by mountains. The pilot had the controls on the dashboard, and Joe was sitting next to him with a handheld GPS. He kept telling the pilot they were too low, but the pilot thought they were fine because the radar altimeter would go off if they were too low.

Joe kept telling him it was about to be a problem, but the pilot wasn't worried—until they started to see hills and trees in front of them and the lights of the valley beyond. The pilot asked to see the handheld and said, "Oh shit!" The radar altimeter had malfunctioned.

The point of the story is to show that if you do not have good gauges, you'll probably one day crash. And if you are flying around with no gauges at all, you are definitely going to crash. You always need a sense of your surroundings, so you don't make mistakes or plow into a mountain.

> YOU ALWAYS NEED A SENSE OF YOUR SURROUNDINGS, SO YOU DON'T MAKE MISTAKES OR PLOW INTO A MOUNTAIN.

Your numbers are the gauges for your business. Not knowing your numbers is like flying your helicopter without navigation.

You Need to Charge More

You can probably think of a lot of excuses. "I need to have at least twenty-five years in business before I can charge more." Or, "The guy down the block isn't charging that much. I'll lose jobs." Or, "I just need more clients."

This mindset is holding you back. The going rate is going to kill your business. Most contractors care too much about what the other guy is charging when it's not even relevant. Your numbers are different from theirs.

You should have confidence in your skill and charge what it is worth. Stop letting your business model screw you. **Remember, you don't need MORE clients. You need BETTER clients.** And to get the better clients, you must have a better business.

Crabs In a Bucket

It can be hard to initiate change when your family members or peers in the business don't seem to support it. This reminds me of the story of the crabs in a bucket.

A man was walking along the beach and saw another man fishing in the surf with a bait bucket beside him. As he drew closer, he saw that the bait bucket had live crabs inside but no lid.

"Why don't you cover your bait bucket, so the crabs won't escape?" he asked.

The man replied, "If there is one crab in the bucket, it would surely crawl out very quickly. When there are many crabs in the bucket, if one tries to crawl up the side, the others grab ahold of it and pull it back down so that it will share the same fate as the rest of them."

The moral of this story: Ignore the crabs you have in your life. Recognize who they are, even if they are the people you love the most—and ignore them.

Charge ahead and do what is right for you. It may not be easy, and you may not succeed as much or as quickly as you'd like. Regardless, you will never share the same fate as those who never try.

Sometimes if a person tries to do something differently to improve themselves or dream big, others will try to drag them back down like the crabs to share their fate at the bottom. They may even think they have the best of intentions, trying to protect you from failure. In reality, they are holding you back.

You must do what is right for you, win or lose. Whether you succeed or fail, you will never have the same fate as those who never tried.

How many times have you been the victim of the crabs in a bucket mentality? Commit now to never letting it happen again. Get going, and climb out of that bucket!

CHAPTER 4

SMALL CHANGES, BIG IMPACT

When you own and run a business, you wear a lot of hats. When you already feel like you're working 24/7, it's hard to think about changing anything. You can't find the time to think about it, much less put a change in place.

There are several small steps to take that can make a surprisingly big difference in the way your business runs and profits. Let's talk about a few fairly easy changes for some quick wins.

Lessons from a Dishwasher

You don't have to perfect your system before you start improving it. The most time-saving business system can be as simple as washing dishes!

Think about something you do efficiently outside of your business, and then model a business process after it. For instance, the way we handle the dishes in our house is quite similar to how I run certain systems in my business.

Our thirteen-year-old loads the dishwasher, and then our five-year-old empties it when the dishes are clean, but he doesn't know where everything goes. We have specific places on the counter for him to place the dishes once he pulls them from the dishwasher.

After that, our nine-year-old daughter helps him put the dishes into their correct places. The five-year-old can't do it all alone, and it would take the nine-year-old too long to do it all by herself. But together, they make a great team, and they get it done. That's the system.

This means that my wife and I are not involved in loading or unloading at all. If one child isn't available to complete the assigned task, it's not a major setback for my wife or me to jump in and handle just that one part since the other two children are still involved.

This system in our house takes the pressure off my wife and me. I am glad we have our kids involved in this household task because the dishes need to get done, and my wife and I have more important family duties to tackle. We are better able to run the household when we are free—mentally and physically—from menial tasks that can actually be completed by others. There are family tasks that cannot be planned or executed by anyone other than us, and intentionally removing ourselves from the simple tasks allows us to focus on what only we can do for our family.

Think about an efficient system you have outside your business that you can use to inspire a business system you need. Figure out what duties you can (and should) remove yourself from. Then, consider who has the particular qualifications or capabilities to get the job done. There are other tasks in your business that only you as the leader can complete, and you need the mental time and space to plan and execute those tasks. Getting even one job off your plate can make a difference in the amount of stress and pressure you feel.

Think about the items below. Can any (or all) of them be handed off to another member of the team to free up your time for the bigger things?

- ❑ Maintaining subcontractor list
- ❑ Answering phone calls
- ❑ Checking emails
- ❑ Writing the end-of-job punch list
- ❑ Updating vendor price lists
- ❑ Selecting and updating software

Make Sure to Use the Right Numbers

There are two more numbers that you need to understand and file away in your head—markup and margin. Understanding the difference between the two is extremely important.

I know this can be confusing. I used to be confused by it as well. But too often, when contractors talk about markup, they are actually referring to the margin of profit on their jobs. They then use that percentage when they mark up their next job. If you use these terms incorrectly, you might be setting a price on your jobs that is too high or too low, which can result in lost sales and profits. I have forms on my website to help you figure this out. Think of it this way:

Markup

Markup is the amount by which the cost of a job is increased in order to calculate a selling price. With a markup of 41%, a bathroom remodel that costs $7,000 would add an additional $2,870 to yield a total price of $9,870. Easy, right?

$7,000 + 41% markup = $9,870

Profit Margin

Profit margin is the gap (or difference) between your costs and the price of goods or services being sold. In our above example, with a $9,870 price to the client, the margin (or difference) is $2,870. This $2,870 difference between your costs and what the customer pays is also your profit margin. But what's the percentage?

$2,870 ÷ $9,870 = 29%

This is where it can get tricky. To calculate your profit percentage, you need to divide the profit amount ($2,870) by the job cost ($9,870) which results in a 29% profit margin. The 29% profit margin is different than the markup amount, and that's where problems can occur. If you incorrectly use your 29% margin (profit) as your markup number, you could price the job at $9,030 and lose $840. Over time that adds up.

What if you consistently did this? How much money would you be leaving on the table? Over several jobs, it starts to add up. If this is something you've been doing, don't beat yourself up. We don't know what we don't know. Just start fresh tomorrow. You can also get help by downloading The Profitable Contractor Toolbox from my website at **OneYearRescuePlan.com**.

Zig Ziglar used to say, "That guy is walking around with my money in his pocket." You must mark up your costs enough to cover your expenses and have a net profit at the end. This is important to understand, and it's an easy thing to fix. Let's get you the profits you deserve on your next job.

Proposal Fees

A few other small changes can help you jump-start the change your business needs. Proposals are one place to start. Here are two thoughts:

- It's okay to charge prospects to write proposals.
- Proposals are not estimates.

First things first, yes, **you can charge for a proposal**. I know it can be frightening to ask a potential client for money before you do physical work for them. But think about it. They have just asked you for a bid/proposal that requires a fair amount of work. And time is money. We don't get our time back, so we need to protect it as much as possible. Your experience and knowledge have value. Lawyers, doctors, and accountants get paid for answering questions. Why shouldn't a contractor?

> MY FIRST PAID PROPOSAL WAS JUST $50.

I'll be honest—my first paid proposal was just $50. I had to start somewhere. My business coach told me to ask for the fee up front—over the phone, before even meeting the prospect. I did not feel comfortable with that, so that first time, I decided to talk to the customer face to face. I wanted to be able to see their body language and gauge their reaction so I would feel more comfortable doing it over the phone the next time.

I don't think the words left my mouth confidently at that first meeting. This was new for me and was pushing me way outside my comfort zone. You need to know that this is totally normal and should be expected.

But after that first time, I have never looked back. My proposal fee has increased, and they can be upwards of $500, depending on the scope of the project. This fee not only allows me to generate a little extra income, but it also allows me to prequalify my clients. I wish I had been taught this many years ago, but I try not to look back too much. The past is the past, and we are going to create a new future for you.

Another thing to remember is that **a proposal is not an estimate**. I didn't fully appreciate this, and it's one of the most important things I want you to understand.

Estimates are based on an educated guess that comes from your previous experience. If you are calling vendors and researching products specific to a prospect's job, you are doing more than estimating. This is a proposal.

This helped me understand the value a proposal brings to the table. And if you aren't already, I would strongly encourage you to start using the word proposal.

> THE PAST IS THE PAST, AND WE ARE GOING TO CREATE A NEW FUTURE FOR YOU.

You are actually doing work for this client, so they should not have a problem paying a small fee upfront for the time you will invest in trying to give them accurate numbers and a plan for their project. If they do object, chances are you will encounter friction during the job, so that should be a major red flag.

By establishing trust with a client and identifying a budget early on, you can generate a solid proposal and establish a clear, mutually beneficial path forward.

That seemingly small $50 fee I asked for changed my business forever. I still remember how uncomfortable I felt during that first conversation, even though I spent much more than $50 worth of my time writing that proposal. But I wanted to be sure they saw the value of the proposal and that I earned their money.

We made another appointment to discuss the job, and I presented them with the numbers. Within a few minutes, I had the job scheduled and a check for $50 plus a deposit of half the job. I felt like I had just won the lottery.

When you implement this strategy, you'll quickly find that most prospects will respond in one of three ways:

1. They have no problem with the proposal fee. You write the proposal, present it to them, and **you get paid for it.** They understand they are paying for your professional knowledge and experience. This also helps establish trust with them, and you often get a signed contract and deposit.
2. You do not get a signed contract for the job, but you still get paid for the time you spent developing the proposal. Not a big win, but you didn't give your valuable time away.
3. This might be the most useful outcome. You screened this client during the phone call. They thought it was nonsense for you to charge a fee for a proposal when "everyone else is doing them for free." This short call gives you valuable information. If they aren't willing to pay a small fee for your expertise, you can guess how future transactions will go with them. This prospect is not

your ideal client. You've just saved yourself from wasting time and energy with them. BOOM.

Small changes can have a big impact. Charging for proposals forever changed how I run my business and helped me see the value I bring to every project and my clients. As I said, I've never looked back. I now vet all clients over the phone. During the first conversation, I tell prospects about my proposal fee—just like my business coach instructed. I then try to determine whether we would be a good fit and able to work together. If we are, then great. If we aren't, that's okay too. Remember, if we work for everyone, we work for no one.

Setting up this new process was my first step on the way to better clients. Sometimes a bad client might sneak in, like weeds in the garden. But I immediately eliminate them from my top client list and move on. I learn something every time, which improves the processes, and makes that type of client less likely to get past me in the future.

The only way to achieve higher profits and revenue is to figure out who your top client is. Through my One-Year Rescue Plan, I'll work with you using proven methodologies and strategies to help identify top clients and find more of them.

You might think this all sounds really hard, if not impossible. But remember that "big doors swing on small hinges." Small changes can lead to big opportunities. You've got little to lose and a lot to gain, and I can help get you where you want to be.

I know you can do this!

Quick Business Wins

There have been a lot of references to identifying your top or ideal client. Don't worry. We're going to talk about the right way to do that in the upcoming chapters.

But here are two quick tips to start getting better clients right now:

Prequalify your next prospect by implementing a one-hour consultation fee. This sets you up as a professional from the start. Remember, in the beginning, some prospects will not be on board with this new process in your business. But you don't want all of your old clients anyway. Some of them have been dragging you down. If they won't pay for your professional advice on a project that will last for years, they are probably not a win for your business.

Address the scope and budget of the project up front. The best way to serve your clients is to have an understanding of what the project will require and what their approximate budget is. The best plans are developed when both parties are in sync.

The client needs to be clear about what they want and what they expect the final bill to be. As a professional, you need to make sure they understand what it will take to get from start to finish. Clear communication during this first step is of utmost importance. It's essential to agree on the scope of the project, what it will cost, and/or what their budget can afford. This will help get that top client on board and ensure a smooth project.

Stop Fooling Yourself

How many times have you said to yourself, "I will make it up on the next job," or even better, "I will make it up on the next project for that SAME client"? Really think about that. I hope you see how that sounds kind of ridiculous. If you can't make the current job profitable, then how the hell are you going to make the next one any better, let alone make up for the profit you lost?

I apologize if I seem a little blunt, but it's just not realistic. Sometimes you have to cut your losses and say no. I know it's hard to turn down work, but there will be other work.

Even during a pandemic or recession, when a lot of people are struggling, there will be jobs. There is always work. You are surrounded by it, and the right customers are out there looking for you!

With those quick fixes to get you started, we will now do a deep dive into identifying and getting top clients. To level up your business, this is probably the most important step to take.

Begin by asking yourself:

- What are you doing right now to attract the clients you want to work for?
- What steps can you take to start looking for them? Where might your top clients be?

Don't wait for better clients to show up. Understand who they are and then find them. Let's get started!

CHAPTER 5

THE RIGHT CLIENTS ARE THE KEY

I had just committed to a small remodeling job for repeat clients, Mike and Katie Smith. This was the third time I had worked with them, and their parents were also clients of mine. For this project, Mike and Katie had a tight timeframe because they were expecting a new baby, and the due date was fast approaching.

I fit the project into my packed calendar and expected it to be pretty straightforward. A few hours after starting the project, however, I noticed a horrible cat urine smell. The stench was foul and only intensified as more drywall dust hit the ground. What had started as a quick remodel involving drywall repair, trim work, new flooring, and paint was turning into a bigger project. Sound familiar?

I knew I couldn't complete the project without addressing this issue, which meant more time and cost. I was going to have to amend the proposal because of these unforeseen circumstances.

We've all been in this situation, and it's tough. As I gave the Smiths the revised proposal, I could only hope they would understand. They couldn't bring a newborn baby home to construction work (let alone a smelly, half-completed project). Luckily, they immediately realized the predicament and agreed to the price increase. We all laughed about the bizarre cat urine smell and moved on. You can see why the entire Smith family falls into my ideal customer category.

After finishing the Smith's project, I realized I wanted more clients like Mike and Katie. Repeat customers always rank highly in my book, but it was more than that. I wanted customers who respect and value my expertise, who communicate well, and who understand that unexpected costs are part of the remodeling process. The big question was—where would I find these ideal clients?

Luckily, I discovered, they were closer than I thought.

The Right Clients

Finding the right clients is a game-changer. They are great to work with and make your life much happier and easier—answering calls promptly, working with you (not against you!) to set plans, asking good questions, and appreciating your expertise.

You take care of the clients you love to work with! They value the service you provide, and you want more of them, don't you? There is one slight problem. **Bad clients get in the way of providing the good clients with the attention and focus they deserve**. The path to the right clients means you have to get rid of the wrong clients—the ones who don't want to pay you what you're worth and who cause lots of problems along the way.

To get started, let's figure out what makes the right clients. Think about the clients you've loved working with (not the ones who make you cringe when their names show up on caller ID) and answer the following questions:

- Who would you list as your top five clients?
- Which clients are you most excited to work with?
- What qualities or characteristics do these clients have in common?
- How much revenue did these clients generate for your business?

Now, go through your client list from the past twelve months, and list your top six revenue-generating clients. Are any clients on both lists? You're starting to create your ideal client list.

For a more in-depth Client Assessment review, go to my website—**OneYearRescuePlan.com**.

Red Flags

After starting a list of top clients, you may wonder how to find new ones. It's actually pretty easy. A lot of clients tell you exactly who they are and how they're going to behave—you just have to pay attention. Over the years, I've found this out the hard way.

Here's a list of just some of the red flags to watch out for:

- **Rude Behavior**
  Respect. Some things are non-negotiable, like respect. You treat clients with respect, and they treat you with respect. Period. End of discussion. If someone is a jerk (especially with money involved), you know to do one thing—run. Run far and run fast.

- **The "Why Don't You Sharpen Your Pencil" Customer**
  This type of customer only looks at the bottom line. They try to nickel and dime you on pricing. Working with these folks doesn't allow you to grow your business in a way that you need and deserve.

- **Something's Off**
  You have a gut feeling, instinct, or intuition that something's not quite right. There's no need to overthink it or get another opinion. You just know. Trust your intuition. It will likely help you avoid unhealthy clients and situations. While this is not a foolproof method to avoid rotten clients, it is definitely a great indicator!

Time-Wasters

Looking back, I now realize that my old system wasn't a system. **It was survival**. I was constantly scrambling behind the scenes to land clients, writing proposals for everything that came my way. The tail was wagging the dog, and I was missing out on what was important to me—time spent with my family doing things I loved to do.

The only thing that could change this situation was me. I had to commit to change and a new way of doing things—no more blaming a project or pointing fingers at others involved.

I remember one time I missed my wedding anniversary dinner because I was writing up a proposal. It was a new low, even for me, but the story didn't end there. After resubmitting the bid and lowering the numbers, I never heard from the guy again. I tried calling and left a few messages—no response. A couple of months later, I ran into him at Costco. Typically, I do not address business in public. I think it's bad manners. But I was frustrated by the situation. He, at first, acted like he hadn't seen me. When I said hello and asked about the build, he said they were choosing contractors that week. This was news to me, and it was a big fat lie. It was the last I heard from him, and they continued with the building of their new home.

> I DON'T LET MY PROSPECTS' PROBLEMS BECOME MY PROBLEMS.

I guess the happy ending to this story is that it pushed me over the edge. I was done with timewasters and ready to change. I will never get back the time I wasted on him, but the pain it caused forced me to realize that I needed a change.

With the policies I now have in place, this situation would never have happened. Now:

- I don't let my prospects' problems become my problems.
- If a prospect is not able to pay my prices, then it is very clear to me that we probably won't have a great working relationship, and I usually pass on the project.
- I have certain service fees in place, so I can address my prospects' needs early on in the process.
- A client must wait until my schedule opens up for their project to start. I no longer squeeze someone in on a Saturday or work late evenings.
- I am always upfront and honest with my prospect.

I now prescreen my clients during what I call the "Don't Waste Your Time" phone call. Doing this phone call correctly tells you within the first few minutes whether the opportunity is worth pursuing.

Following are a *couple* of examples of the kinds of questions I typically ask on the prescreening call:

"When are you looking to have the project completed, and is there any flexibility with this? AND "When do you plan to start the project?"

This question is so important. If you know you are not able to meet their deadline, do not try to squeeze it into your schedule. Having the right jobs are the key to your success. If you try to squeeze this client in, they might be appreciative up front, but troubles often lie around the corner. Some prospects may indicate they are in a hurry, but in reality, they are months away from starting because of the many details that need to be sorted out before the demo begins.

"What is your budget or spending plan for the project?"

Some prospects want you to guess at this number. What good does this do you—or the prospect? You want to point your prospect in the right direction. So, it is necessary to understand the budget so you can make an informed decision. I get it. These prospects may think the only reason you are asking about their budget is so you can maximize what you are charging them. Red Flag. If this is the case, they are not your ideal client. If they think you are taking them to the cleaners at this stage, then the financial talks along the way are only going to get more uncomfortable.

Maybe they want granite countertops but are unaware this will take them outside their budget. By addressing this early on, you can see how flexible and realistic they are. Are they willing to make some sacrifices for their project, or are they counting on you to just make it happen?

In addition to their budget, another thing I will frequently ask prospects to do is send some pictures of the project area—either by email or text. These must be submitted before we discuss the project any further.

When I ask a prospect to send pictures, I am looking for a couple of things. First, do I really want the job? A prospect can sugarcoat things over the phone. But, as they say, a picture is worth a thousand words. Once you review the pictures, you may realize that this client and/or job will be a pain that you just don't want or need.

It also gives me a clue about whether or not they can follow directions. Sending you a few pictures sounds so simple, right? But you'd be surprised at how hard it is sometimes. If they can't do this one relatively easy thing, it's likely that communication will be a challenge, and that makes the whole project hard.

After our initial discussions, if we both choose to proceed, I will either write up a paid proposal or schedule a paid onsite consultation visit. I always get some form of payment up front. Clients are getting a personalized proposal and should value your work and time enough to pay for a consultation (even before the hammer hits the first nail).

Right Clients Improve Your Life

If you don't get the right clients, you will not only be miserable but also closer to broke. That's right. Getting the right clients improves your bottom line. The industry norm preaches that knowing your numbers is the only way to become profitable, but that's only one part of the equation. Having the right clients gets you across the finish line and rolling it in.

Of course, you should know your numbers so well that when a prospect contacts you about a job, you can quickly give an accurate estimate. But you also have to be prepared for the next step—working with clients. Once an estimate is created, many potential clients want to negotiate. Maybe they can't afford the estimate and want you to lower your prices. At this point, you need to stay strong. You know your numbers. Don't sell yourself short.

Now, think about the last time you lowered your price when a client asked you to "sharpen your pencil." We have all had that customer and that job. What was the job and price you proposed? How much did you lower your price? Write down your answers below—and be honest.

_____
_____
_____
_____
_____
_____

This customer probably said that you would get the job if you just worked on the numbers a little. Such an approach degrades your value both financially and professionally. You know your numbers and your business. Clients who are constantly asking for lower prices are not the top clients you want.

I get it. It feels crazy to turn down jobs. For a long time, my fees were extremely low, and I ended up saying yes to multiple jobs to keep my schedule filled. When you are a small operation, multiple jobs paying peanuts is a setup for disaster. And, even worse, these low-paying projects and bad customers are stealing your time and lowering your value. It can be easy to allow these kinds of projects and customers to take over your schedule, but we're not going to let that happen anymore.

Keys to Success

The keys to success are simple—know your value and choose to work with the right clients. That's it. Knowing your value means you bill what you're worth. It also means that you deliver on your price by providing excellent work and quality customer service. Your exceptional skills and service allow you to charge top dollar.

Clients who can't (or don't want to) pay for your worth should not be on your list. They are not the right clients. Please stay strong, my friend. If someone tries to negotiate on your price, remember, it will not end there. They will try to nickel and dime you in other areas of the job. You are the expert in your field, and you need to be paid for it.

Right Clients = Right Revenue

The right clients can improve your bottom line, so it's time to look at your client list and get rid of the customers who don't value your skills. Yes, get rid of them. They will drain you completely and add unnecessary stress in your life. The below chart will help you figure out which clients to keep and which ones to let go of.

Client Review Checklist

1. Sort your clients by the revenue generated.
2. Give them a smiley or frowny face, based on what it's like to work with them.
3. Jot down some traits (e.g., estimated income, where they work, what they drive, what upsets them, education level, etc.).

Clients	Revenue and Hourly Return	☺ or ☹	Common Traits
1)			
2)			
3)			
4)			
5)			

To get more information on identifying non-paying customers, go to **OneYearRescuePlan.com**, where you can download my free report, "**7 Signals to Identify Non-Paying Customers**." You might be surprised how familiar these customers sound.

Now, look at the above clients. Which clients generate high revenue and have a smiley face? These are the folks you want to keep, and you want more of them! See how easy that was? You've figured out which clients are great to work with and value your worth. They are the ones who understand if changes are needed and are flexible when the inevitable unexpected event comes up, such as a delay on materials delivery due to unforeseen circumstances, or lack of manpower due to illness. It is so much fun serving these clients.

Right Clients Are The Golden Ticket

The path to the right clients means getting rid of the wrong clients and knowing your own value. Focusing on the right clients creates a foundation for success in your business and your life. You're choosing to work with people who want to pay you what you're worth and who respect and value your contribution. The best part? The right clients improve both the quality of your work life and your company's bottom line. They will put your business into overdrive.

CHAPTER 6

HOW TO GET TOP CLIENTS: BASIC

Have you noticed that you usually do things the hard way and then figure out what works? The same here. Let me tell you a story of how I actually did things (for far too long) and how I've changed my ways. For the record, I'm much happier now.

It was a rainy Saturday morning when I pulled up to a driveway lined across with Home Depot buckets full of sand. I was meeting Fred and Clare Johnson, who wanted me to redo their family's upstairs bathroom. I was eager for the work, and they were desperate to get it done. They had heard that I was reasonably priced and did excellent work.

Strike #1. You know what reasonably priced means, right? It means you're cheaper than the other contractors out there. To earn a profit, you need to charge what you're worth and deliver.

I wanted to get the job and get it started, so I set up a Saturday meeting.

Strike #2. I should have waited until Monday to contact the client to discuss the project and proposal. Top clients won't be available on weekends because they're spending time with their families.

But, here I was, in the Johnsons' living room, and they could sense that I wanted to land the job. Just to be clear, we hadn't even discussed their budget. I had created a rough proposal for them based on very general numbers, and they had a few questions. Fred asked about a couple of specific line items and questioned the pricing on something with a very tight profit margin. He asked, "Can you sharpen up the numbers on the shower tile?"

Strikes #3 and #4. Always know a customer's budget before writing a proposal. Always. And, remember that you know your numbers and profit margins. Working within a customer's budget is professional and expected. Changing numbers to fit their budget leaves you stuck with the cost and potentially unpaid.

I knew what the job would cost but didn't want to lose a new customer. So I headed home and back to the kitchen table, where I calculated a few more figures and found a way to save a few hundred dollars off a proposal that was already fairly tight.

Strike #5. Proposals are meant to list project costs, not to give customers the lowest number. Your prospect might love your low numbers, but you will hate the job. And worse, the job won't be profitable.

As my Saturday disappeared, I rationalized the new price. I thought, "It will be worth it. These are new customers who will love my work and be great referrals." Have you ever had those thoughts?

I wish I could say this was a one-off, but sadly, it wasn't. This was me and my life. Honestly, I had no life, only work. My marriage was on the rocks from all the weekends spent crunching numbers and meeting with clients. My credit cards were maxed out from the gap between buying supplies and getting paid. And all this stress led to horrible eating habits and weight gain. My brain was overloaded, and I could not think straight. This was the old way.

You don't want the old way anymore because it screams crappy clients and NO profit.

You are in business because you are GREAT at your craft. Your business needs you to be profitable as well. Running a profitable business is key, and I will tell you time and time again, working for better clients is a must. **If you allow the clients to be in control of the job ... you just lost.**

I am not saying you lost the job altogether. But you did lose in the fact that you just took on a client who does not understand what it takes to run a successful, profitable construction business. Not a great starting point.

So let's get started with your new approach to getting only the best clients.

Know Your Brand

You are good at what you do. You offer something valuable. But that doesn't mean much if your clients don't know what value you bring to a project. By clearly defining your company's brand, you're creating an image. You're telling customers who you are, what you do, and most importantly, what sets you apart from the other guys. Do you offer better customer service? Better on-time project completion rates? It can be anything, but it needs to be a message that is clear and meaningful to your customers.

You don't have to figure this out alone. A coach or mentor can help you see things that might not be obvious to you. Have you heard the expression, "You can't read the label when you're inside the jar."? Getting a different perspective can help you see what is actually possible. How many times have you heard another contractor say, "We already know what works," and "We tried that before, and it didn't work"?

Sometimes groundbreaking ideas do not come from seasoned contractors in your field, but rather from people with different backgrounds and expertise who can help you look at situations from an "out-of-the-jar" perspective, especially when that business growth strategist has been in your shoes before.

Build Value

When building your client base, you need to focus on getting better clients. Not just more clients—better clients. You'll get better clients when you can differentiate your company from others—when you can provide an added value. This is not value added to your financial statements. This is your opportunity to add value to the customer experience.

> NOT JUST MORE CLIENTS—
> BETTER CLIENTS.

That's why when I say value, I'm not talking about pricing. The value I'm talking about is what you sets you apart when doing projects. What is special about you and your company? If you don't differentiate your business by publicizing your value, you will be competing with others based only on price. That is a race to the bottom and not one you want to be in.

Building value creates other benefits that will make your life easier. When customers are motivated to have you (and only you), it's easier to collect payment up front for consulting on projects or writing proposals. Customers may want to be put on your schedule before a proposal is even written, and it will be standard to collect a 50% down payment when a project starts. The list goes on and on. None of these benefits requires you to give prospects anything and everything before they decide whether to pay you or not. That is total nonsense!

Under Promise and Over Deliver

Some people may disagree with the idea that you should under promise and over deliver, but they probably don't work in construction. Every project involves countless workers, multiple deliveries, and inevitable delays. I've found that it's best to set realistic (if a bit slow) timelines.

For instance, if you say you will have a proposal to them in two days and it takes you two and a half days, then you failed on your promise. But, if you say it will take you two weeks and one week later you make an appointment to go over the proposal, you look better and better to them.

Work to be more realistic about how much time will be needed to get a project finished. You may need to explain that it's likely to take six to eight weeks to finish due to trade partner schedules and weather. But, if everything lines up and you finish in four and a half weeks, then you will be the "golden" contractor.

Think about the opposite. If you've said something will take four weeks, and it finishes in four and a half weeks, those clients are likely to remember that you did not keep your promise on the completion date.

So, in the contracting business, when we say under promise and over deliver—it's a great idea.

Understand Marketing

Marketing is more than printing out business cards and slapping a logo on your truck. It's everything you do—from how you present yourself to how you get the job done. Do you show up to a job in a filthy truck that hasn't been washed in weeks? You probably want to rethink that one.

Do you answer calls promptly? Is your business logo on your shirts and hats? You want to develop brand loyalty, so customers recognize who you are and what you deliver. The best part of marketing? You already have the best marketing tool available—your customers! Their positive experience can help you market your company by providing testimonials and referrals.

Get Testimonials

You definitely have clients who love your work and only have the very best things to say about you and their completed project. These are messages that your potential clients need to hear (and one of your most powerful marketing tools). How do you currently collect testimonials from past clients? I suggest making it part of your business process to get feedback from your clients. You can use their testimonials and get their thoughts on how to improve your business. Win-win!

Ask for Client Referrals

Referrals can be tricky. You definitely want them, but honestly, you only want them from your top clients. Think of different ways you can encourage and reward existing clients who refer new customers.

Stick with the New Process

Are you getting this? You don't need to slash prices and work weekends to get clients. When you take this new approach, you'll get better clients—the kind of clients who value your work and want to pay you what you're worth. All you have to do is commit to changing your ways and stick with it. Don't lapse into old habits that don't get you anywhere. Roll up your sleeves, and get started.

CHAPTER 7

HOW TO PRICE YOUR SERVICES: NEXT LEVEL

I get a bad feeling in the pit of my stomach when I think about how little I valued my time in the past. When I was just starting my business, I let everyone else control what I did and when. From client meetings (at their convenience) to project start dates (based on everyone else's schedules), I felt like I had to do everyone's bidding just to get ahead. Even though I was the boss, **my time and energy were the things that adapted to every situation**, and most of the time I spent on a project was something I didn't even add to the bill.

Not anymore.

With the help of my business coach, I finally got the courage to step up and set terms that match my value. I'm not unreasonable or difficult. I just recognize my worth and made two simple changes. I started actively organizing my schedule to maximize how my time was spent, and I expected to be paid more for the value I bring to my clients and their projects. My time is just as valuable as it was before, but now I'm getting paid three to four times more for it.

What Is Your Time Worth?

We have many demands on our time. Getting projects done and hustling for more work are generally the top two, but what are we forgetting? You got it—that thing you least like to do—managing day-to-day business demands, like pricing.

I constantly hear from my coaching clients that there isn't much they can do about their prices. They're too busy. And besides, the industry sets the numbers.

That's where this book (and a business coach) can help you. You need to quantify your value. It can be tough to buck the system and place a higher price tag on your time. But one thing is certain. **If you keep doing the exact same things, you are going to get the exact same results (and the exact same income).**

Many of you probably set up a pricing system ages ago and have just let it ride ever since. That's easy to do. Working a job and getting new clients takes work and can quickly fill up every hour of your day. But ignoring the management piece of your business is like closing a door on a room full of money. There's a lot of potential just waiting for you to tap into it. Are you ready to open that door?

A story comes to mind that illustrates the consequences of not tapping into your value and the results that are possible when you do!

A Former Idaho Tile "Contractor"

Dustin had the mindset that physical labor meant profit. He was stuck in this mentality for many years, when one day, his grandma said to him, "Grandson, I am so proud of the tile contractor you have become."

All these years, he had just thought of himself as someone who set or installed tile. Hearing the word "contractor" associated with his work seemed out of place—too professional or expert for what he did.

He started in his trade as an apprentice, viewed as a "knuckle dragger." He was the guy who washed the buckets, mixed the mud, shoveled the sand and cement, and was paid an hourly or piece rate to do his job.

Fast forward to ten years later. He started his own business and was trying to survive on piece rate and managing time by the hour. Quickly, he came to the realization that no one paid him for all the things he did (and time that was required) to make a job successful—drive to jobs, pick up materials, write bids, give estimates, do his bookkeeping, etc.

It was at this point that he realized he was not actually running a business—he was still a laborer getting paid a piece rate. And then he remembered his Grandma's words. She had seen him as a contractor.

It was time to start living up to those words. He changed his mindset and started adding other fees, like trip charges, delivery charges, and change order fees. He was beginning to understand the value of his time and expertise.

When he hit his thirties, he realized he also had to think about the money he needed to earn in order to support his family. A good friend asked him at one point, "How much do you actually make?" When the thirty-something tile contractor provided his answer, his friend pushed again, asking, "No, how much do you make? How much do you pay yourself?" This was the first time the tile contractor realized that, up to this point, he had not ever paid himself.

He was paying for his materials, equipment, tools, workers, etc. And he took home whatever was left over. He had never set an amount he actually wanted to make for himself. His friend's questions about what he took home started to change his mentality, and he was reminded of his grandma's statement from years before—how proud she was that he was a tile contractor.

Thanks to his friend (and his grandma), he began to think about the value of his time and started to understand that as a business owner, he could not just be charging for materials. His expertise had tremendous value. He now had a vision of how much money he wanted to make each year. As a result, his perspective of himself changed, and he went from viewing himself as a laborer to selling himself as an experienced business owner. He started getting paid what he was worth, and his whole life improved. This was his biggest light-bulb moment, and he wondered how he had missed this for all those years.

Running Your Business

It's tough. I get that. No one is out there teaching contractors how to run a profitable, sustainable business. Workers are taught how to pound nails, cut and measure things, how to make things plumb, level, and square. They are taught how to work smart and be efficient, and how to be more successful themselves—today, tomorrow, and the next day.

But contractors running their own business don't typically get business management help on how to be profitable. Much of what we know about business is learned on the fly in the midst of finishing projects, getting kids to school, and writing proposals.

Fair Pricing

Early in my career, I had a phenomenal mentor, Bill. He was a great guy with thirty-plus years of experience and a true understanding of how to get a job done and done well. Bill's combination of expertise and experience was priceless. His customers loved his work, and his schedule was packed nine months ahead. You know what else? He charged $25 per hour.

Scratching your head? Yeah. Me, too. Bill could have easily commanded $100 or more per hour but had capped his rate at a measly $25. Perhaps he had an "it's always been done this way" mentality. Or maybe he incorrectly assumed that no one would pay him more than that. Maybe he always wanted to raise his prices but simply didn't know how to make that change a reality.

Whatever the issue was, his rates got in my head and became a fear, especially when I realized that $25 per hour wasn't going to cut it for me, my family, or my business goals. As I considered raising my rates, I wondered how I could justify charging three times what Bill was charging.

I started to realize that while Bill had taught me industry best practices (hammer and nail practices, of course), he couldn't teach me how to run a successful, profitable business. It was difficult for me to see this at the time, but he was merely trading time for money. All I could see was that he had so much work waiting for him, and clients were seeking him out rather than the other way around. This must be the path to success!

But the real story was that each job was a placeholder. Bill was always robbing Peter to pay Paul. Later, I found out his mortgage, electric bills, and insurance always followed him closely, month to month, leaving no room to spare.

I got my courage up and increased my prices from $25 to $35 per hour. I was stuck there for some time. It was a mental block. Once I started working with my business coach, I did not look back. He helped me analyze my pricing structure, and I went from $35 to $72 per hour pretty much overnight. Of course, I missed out on other job opportunities. But there will always be opportunities, and you cannot fit them all in.

One opportunity I was able to take advantage of was more time doing things outside of work. I took a few golf lessons and started to enjoy some nights out on the town with my wife. My mind felt clear, and bad clients were literally being kicked to the curb. I felt good about where my company was, and I was proud to have taken the initiative to make a change.

In the end, I figured out how to sell jobs at a profitable price. I was able to work less and still maintain a very similar revenue. Raising my prices allowed me to meet my financial needs and work less.

My business coach helped me understand what I needed to charge, so I could have some breathing room and more profitable jobs. For me, I went all in. My markup was consistently at 41%. Sometimes higher. If I did not get a job, it was okay. I would rather work with a client and on a job that was better suited to my business.

Being consistent with how I priced my jobs, and being okay if an opportunity did not work out, were key for me. I felt proud that I finally was able to crack the code on filtering out crappier clients by knowing my numbers and what it took to do a job properly. And that meant charging a fair price that included experience, education, and knowledge in my fees. Only you know what it takes for your business to get the job done correctly. Knowing your numbers makes it easier to figure out what your price needs to be.

Race to the Bottom?

How many conversations have you had with clients that involve price per square foot and what the other guy charges? I would bet too many. It puts you in a spot where you're working up strategies to beat the competition's price, and that is a problem. **It focuses on the wrong thing**. When you start competing on price per square foot, you've joined the race to the bottom, where the winner is the one with the lowest price. Is that really a race you want to win? A project with little or no profit?

Let me make this easy for you. You do NOT want to win that race or work those jobs. You need to ditch this pricing model and get it out of your head. Instead, it's time to start thinking differently.

You want to work with top clients who value what you bring to the project. That means your customer experience has to make you stand out from the competition. I have an especially strong opinion about this because it's something I did not do well in my early years. I learned as I went.

While I felt like customers were lucky to have me on their project, I generally did not do anything special or different to make a project particularly enjoyable for them. Construction is very stressful for everyone, especially if you are the one who is living in it.

Think about what you can do to make your client's life a little bit easier as you work on a project. What can you do to give them a great experience along the way? Are you providing them with the same exact service or product that your buddy or competition down the street is? Are you trying to copy what your competition is doing? Look for ways to differentiate yourself from the pack!

Differentiate Yourself

We are wired to instantly notice something different, and we pay attention until we can identify whether it's an opportunity or a threat. But there is one problem. To really get noticed, you have to stand out in the sea of competition. Your business depends on it.

Think about the following questions:

- What do you do in your business right now that makes you different from your competition?
- What could you start doing to be different?

There are no right or wrong answers here. I just want you to start brainstorming and let your imagination have fun with this. You want a change in your business, right? Let's get to work.

What Are Your BIGGEST Strengths?

- _____
- _____
- _____
- _____
- _____
- _____
- _____
- _____

How Do You Add Value?

Lots of contractors talk about adding value to a project, but what that means is not really clear. Let me make this simple. You want to show clients that you go above and beyond to make the experience great for them and to ensure better results. That's added value. Of course, you're going to do great work, but I challenge you to brainstorm ways below where you can amp up your game and add more value.

- _____
- _____
- _____
- _____
- _____
- _____
- _____
- _____

Immutable Laws

This may seem like a crazy place to start, but you need to know your immutable laws. You are probably wondering what the heck immutable laws are! Well, let me tell you—they are the rules you live by. They define you. They are a blend of ethics, core values, and a self-assigned law—all wrapped up into one. They are the rules we have set and defined for ourselves over the years. Knowing what your unbreakable laws are will help you identify and attract new, top clients.

Let's take a moment to figure out your immutable laws. The list doesn't have to be perfect, and your thinking may change. But a general idea of how you like to operate and what you find acceptable is essential. There is a lot of power behind identifying these immutable laws. You learn what you want and head in that direction.

Think about a project that went really well and one that went pretty badly. What are the rules in life that you never want to break again? Some examples might be:

1. Always be authentic.
2. Never let a client talk you down on the price.
3. Always provide good service.
4. No jerks allowed.

If you want some extra help figuring out your immutable laws, go to **OneYearRescuePlan.com**, where you'll find questionnaires and more that will help you grow your business.

Price Should Match Your Value

You should now have a pretty good idea of how much value you add to every project. It's time you recognize that you're worth a lot more than you realize. Your pricing should match your value—time to forget per-hour pricing figures.

Your value and what you charge should be directly related to the results you provide your clients.

That's a huge shift. Don't think of pricing as an hourly or even project-based number. Think of it as what YOU bring to the table. How many clients love the work you do? How many recognize the expertise you offer? More importantly, do your rates and your profit reflect that?

Here is where you get to think big. You can get to 41%.

More than likely, increasing your markup by 10% today won't cost you any jobs. And if it does, these sure are not the clients you want to keep working for. By increasing your revenue, you just realized higher profits on your next job. And you didn't do anything extra ... except realize your VALUE.

But I want you to think past the 41%. How can you make your business a fun place to work? How can you create so much value, your team members (employees) will stay with you for years? How can you create so much value that you are now thinking about the legacy your business will provide to your family for generations? I want you to think BIG!

Your mind may get in the way. So, when it does, remember why you got in this business to begin with. You wanted freedom, you wanted to be successful, and you definitely wanted to have a profitable business.

Run PROFITABLE Jobs

You've set up systems that help your business run more efficiently AND make you more money. Hopefully, you're starting to prequalify clients and collect fees for writing up job proposals and/or doing consultations.

Now, the rubber hits the road. We need to add profit into the proposal itself, which means understanding the difference between profit and margin. You have a general idea of what this means. But let me give you an example of how it can play out.

Imagine you are working on a proposal for a bathroom gut and redo. First things first: What costs are involved? Think labor, materials, rentals, and/or permits. Once you have those numbers, you add in the markup factor. This is where you're going to start changing things up.

What do you need to make your business profitable?

Maybe you're charging around a 10% markup. That's not enough. The markup should cover the true cost of the project, PLUS how much you need to make to cover your living, and when things go wrong. Something always happens, and you need to cover yourself. You are not ripping people off by planning for the unexpected. The following bar graph compares a 10% markup to one that's 41%.

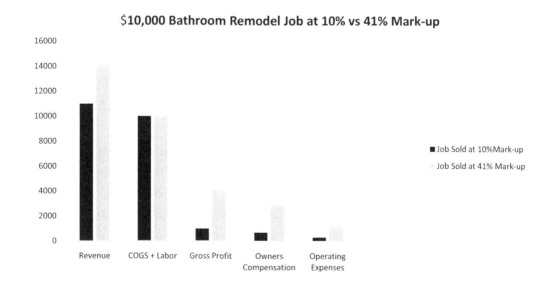

(Note: Owners Compensations includes owners pay, profit and tax.)

While the cost of goods and labor are the same, it's easy to see how big of an impact the right markup (41% vs 10%) can have on revenue, gross profit, owner's compensation and operating expenses. The last two categories are where it counts, leaving you more money to pay yourself and reinvest in your business.

Mark up your jobs enough to support your business and create the lifestyle you desire. Being an entrepreneur is supposed to be satisfying and rewarding. I have one suggestion with whatever markup and gross profit margin you choose. Be consistent. Consistency wins. Consistent small changes will yield big results. So, if a 30% or 40% markup makes you feel uncomfortable, try 20% or 25%. Once you are comfortable selling your jobs at that rate, then raise it some more. Raise it until you feel comfortable with the price you are charging your clients and the revenue you are generating for your business. You need to be profitable in order to be of service to your clients. Don't feel ashamed of making a healthy profit. <u>Businesses that are successful are profitable</u>.

For the past two years, I only do jobs where I can factor in at least a 41% markup. That gives me about a 29% profit margin. That is the lowest multiplier I use. I use it frequently. But there are times where I need to make a higher profit margin, so I adjust accordingly. It allows me to have more flexibility in my decision-making, gives my family a "better me" at home, and allows us to do things as a family that were not possible when I only charged my clients a 10% markup. I was losing the fight for over a decade. Not anymore, my friend. And from here on out, you won't either.

How many jobs each year would you need to do at a higher markup so that you can support your family and lifestyle? Is it five? Ten? Maybe it's fifteen. This is a question only you know the answer to.

And how much nicer would it be to cut down on the number of clients you are working for and still make the revenue and profit that supports your business and lifestyle?

Pricing projects involves more than just listing out line-item charges and adding in a little extra buffer. You need to place a number on what you bring to the equation—essentially, your value. Don't shortchange yourself. Your expertise, experience, and hard work are equally important line items that deserve compensation. Running an extremely profitable business is something that takes work, and you're doing it—every day.

CHAPTER 8

KICK-START YOUR BUSINESS ... NOW

We've covered how to transform your processes, and now you're ready to take the first step to kickstart your business and your life. Everything we've talked about leads to this transformation where you make sure you get the right clients by letting go of the wrong clients. You heard that right. It's time to get rid of the clients and jobs that are making you miserable. For me, taking this one step completely shifted my perspective and helped me finally like my business again.

Many of you may be wary of this step. It doesn't seem to make sense to get rid of clients. And what about the clients you like? It's time to keep the big picture in mind. You don't want just any clients. You want top clients. To make room for these clients, it's time to clear the deck and stop wasting your time on people and projects that stress you out, don't pay well, and don't make you happy.

Yes, sometimes that means letting go of clients you like. Just because you like a client doesn't mean they're good for your business. I still recall the first client I fired back in 2018. I never thought I could tell someone I liked that I could no longer work for them, but I did.

My crew had just finished a job for Bob and Sue. It was a pretty extensive project. We had tiled a backsplash, installed hardwood flooring, replaced the front door, abated an asbestos popcorn ceiling, and then retextured and painted the same area.

I was headed to their house to drop off a complimentary bottle of wine (one of my company's added-value perks) to celebrate the completion of their project, and I was nervous. I was going to tell them that I would no longer work with them.

While I enjoy their company socially, they are not great clients. They would argue and give conflicting instructions on what they wanted to be done. I felt like too much of my on-site time was spent negotiating their differences rather than working on the project. They made my life very difficult.

They loved the craftsmanship of my work. They told me so. But after many tedious complaints, I needed to reevaluate my working relationship with them. It felt like they were nitpicking at things that were out of my control. I was very clear with them in the beginning, and I felt like they ignored our previous conversations.

So, when I arrived at their house, I thanked them for the opportunity to work for them and also for their friendship. But I told them we needed to end our working relationship. Their expectations did not align with mine. They took the news surprisingly well, and afterward, actually referred me to one of their friends. (Fortunately, the prequalification process I had in place kept that prospect off my ideal client list.)

It was this disconnect between people who were my friends and the same people who were difficult clients that helped me realize I only wanted great clients. Sometimes people can be both, but more often than not, they are separate. Fortunately, in this case, it didn't end the friendship. We still sit next to each other at local baseball games and occasionally see each other at social events. There was an understanding that I valued them as friends, but our working relationship had ended.

By choosing not to work with Bob and Sue, I was choosing to work with better clients, the right clients who would tick all the boxes—communicate well, pay well, and appreciate my work.

Don't Be Afraid to Say "No"

There you have it in a nutshell. Let me say it again. Don't be afraid to say "No"! Get rid of clients and jobs that make you miserable and realize that saying "No" might be the single most powerful thing you can do in your business.

Now, you have some tools to make it easier to say no. Vet your clients before you even take on a project. You can do this by using your initial phone call to prequalify and select the clients and projects you want. Remember the things we talked about that should be discussed before committing to move ahead with a proposal (e.g., timeline, budget, having them send you photos of the area). If they have unrealistic expectations or are unwilling to provide any of this information, that's a red flag. You can save yourself time, money, headaches by telling them they're not a good fit during this first conversation.

Your new policy of charging for proposals and consulting may even weed some of these folks out. If they push back on that, you know they're not the type of client you're looking for.

You can do this! You have already started the process. For more details on client assessment, go to **OneYearRescuePlan.com** and download my forms.

In some cases, you may no longer offer a particular type of service (since you've decided to stick to your sweet spot!). In other instances, your higher minimum fees may discourage some clients. Do not feel guilty about these improvements. The right clients will recognize the value and be happy to pay for your services, and that's an easy way to separate those you want to work with from those you don't.

Final Question

Ask yourself this. Are you just open to making a change, or are you ready to start actively make a change now? This question reminds me of how my friend teaches kids in wrestling about being aggressive. When they have a medal in their hands, he teaches them that they *took* it—that they *took* the medal. When they *took* that, they *chose* to take it. They're taking it from someone else. Right? It's a one-on-one, full-contact sport.

No one is going to simply give that medal to them. *Nope*. They cannot get it for just showing up. They have to *choose* to *take* it. What are they willing to do to *take* it?

If kids walk into a wrestling tournament and they have a desired outcome in mind, <u>then the reason they are able to *take* the medal comes from the investment they made in their dedication, training, and hard work</u>. They took the time to get it.

It's the same thing with our time. Are we going to choose to *take* our time and control it, or are we going to allow it to be taken away from us?

My wrestling coach friend likes to ask the kids, "How did you get that medal?" And when they say, "I took it because I chose to," he knows he has coached them well.

So, I'll ask you this: Overall, do you have a profitable contracting business in place so that you can choose to *take* your medal, or do you have a floundering pseudo-business that takes it away from you instead? Which one do you want?

I hope you've decided you're ready to *take* it, so you can start to enjoy a better business and life.

CHAPTER 9

YOU'VE GOT THIS!

Too many of us are not living our dreams because we are living our fears.
—Les Brown, motivational speaker and former state legislator

Sometimes we start things because we're ready, and sometimes we start things because we need to. You picked up this book because you were ready for a change, and now, you need to commit to that change. We've covered the first steps you need to take, and you can do it.

As you prepare for the change, ask yourself how important it is to change your business. How important is it to start attracting better clients and making more money? How important is it to spend more time with your family? How important is it to have clarity on:

- ❏ Being respected
- ❏ Charging what you are worth.
- ❏ Bringing home more money
- ❏ Profiting more on your jobs
- ❏ Creating products that are different from your competition
- ❏ Spending more time with your loved ones
- ❏ Being the leader of your business
- ❏ Creating a meaningful lifestyle
- ❏ Taking your family on deserved vacations
- ❏ Attracting BETTER clients
- ❏ Creating a contracting business that is a great place to work, profitable, and sellable

Step One: Commit to Change

This new approach is likely to feel strange at first. You may feel unqualified to ask for proposal fees. You may doubt whether you can charge more for what you've always done, or you may feel nervous as you hear others talk about the status quo.

That's okay. Changing how you do things can be challenging, but you're ready for it. You've reached a point where things have to change, or you'll continue to be overworked, underpaid, and stressed out. That's why you're ready to commit to making a change—for yourself and your business.

Once you do, you'll be able to overcome the inevitable challenges along the way. You'll see how the changes you're making will improve your business by setting up new systems that let you increase profit AND decrease your time at work.

Remember why you started your business in the first place—to do something you love AND to earn a living.

Step Two: Work with Top Clients

This one is easy—focus on your top clients. Remember that top client assessment list? The people on that list are the customers you want on your calendar. In fact, you should only be working with top clients. The ones who don't argue with you. The ones who extend grace when an obstacle comes up during the job. The ones who pay you on time and recognize what you are worth.

Like you, I stepped out of my comfort zone and did what was uncomfortable. Being uncomfortable allowed me to experience what I never thought was possible, especially since other contractors were doing nothing like this. What I found is that a new spark and energy came from me that encouraged new conversations with prospects that I never had before. These conversations allowed my clients to have better experiences.

Step Three: Have Patience

This isn't going to happen overnight. Set up your systems, stay focused, and be patient. Give the changes time to work, and the opportunities will come up. As you wait, instead of focusing on the bad clients (like many other businesses), focus on the good clients and do the work to keep them happy. Show them the value you bring to every project.

It's doable!

I was once like you, feeling like there had to be something better. But the way I had been taught was not a path to success. I got by for many years, but the real success I was looking for meant I had to change how I approached everything. Once I realized this (with the help of amazing coaches), I was able to improve my skills, and I was on my way.

> THE BOTTOM LINE? IF YOU CAN IMAGINE IT, YOU CAN EXECUTE IT.

The bottom line? If you can IMAGINE it, you can EXECUTE it.

Step Four: Enjoy What's Next

You've put systems in place, decided only to work with top clients, and continued to do the hard work of running your business and serving your clients—every day. The result? Your business and life will be transformed into something that you once again enjoy. It just took you to make it happen!

The question then becomes . . .

Are you ready to become a profitable business?
Are you ready to attract better clients?
Are you ready to spend more quality time with your family?

Get it done. Time is of the essence, and every day you don't take action towards a new life and business is a day that's passed by. Nobody else can do it for you. YOU are the only one standing in your own way.

You are still reading, which makes me think you are curious, intrigued, and ready to leap into new changes in your contracting business. This book has given you a few steps to begin that change. I wanted something better in my contracting career and took active steps to experience something new, different, and life-changing. But I didn't do it alone. I had coaches who guided me along the way, and it was worth every penny. I ended up with better clients, more profit, and more time at home.

The time I invested in myself and my business wasn't easy, but it gave me hope again, and I couldn't be happier with the results. Let me help you get to where I am. It changed my life so much that it's now my passion to help others make positive changes that can open up doors that were never thought possible.

You know it's time. Let's do this!

THANK YOU

Thank you for giving me the opportunity to share my story with you—and for taking the time to invest in yourself and your business. I would love you to share any business stories, personal stories, or thoughts that came to your mind as you were reading this.

What do you feel is the #1 problem in your business, which, if resolved, would create the biggest impact on your business? Email me and let me know. I want to support you through your journey and would love to know what your takeaways were from reading this book.

Email me at steve@24onCenter.com with the subject line, "Rescue" and let me know what business struggle keeps you awake at night.

Business Website: **www.24onCenter.com**
Resources Website: **OneYearRescuePlan.com**
LinkedIn: **https://www.LinkedIn.com/in/SWDale**
Text Me: **208-918-3604**

WANT MY HELP?

The One-Year Rescue Plan will help you:

- **Identify your top clients** and clearly define your ideal client niche.
- **Identify a unique offering** that specifically appeals to your top clients.
- **Attract more top clients** in your contracting business.
- **Create a strategy** that makes your business stand out from the crowd.
- **Know what your VALUE is**, so that you can be profitable.
- **Create systems** that will allow YOU more freedom in your business and life.

**CHANGE YOUR BUSINESS. CHANGE YOUR LIFE.
CREATE YOUR FUTURE!**

OneYearRescuePlan.com
Or get your cell phone out, and scan the QR code:

ABOUT STEVE DALE

Steve Dale is a contractor, entrepreneur, and author who has run a residential remodeling business for thirteen years. He graduated from Lewis-Clark State College with a business degree and is a certified Pumpkin Plan Strategy coach. Steve combines a strong business foundation with an insider's understanding of what it takes to run a successful remodeling company. He transformed his own business using these skills, which fueled his passion for helping other contractors learn how to run a thriving business while still having a life outside of work.

He lives in Lewiston, Idaho, with his wife and three children. In his free time, he enjoys hunting, fishing, exploring the great outdoors, and spending quality time with loved ones. You can learn more about Steve and download free resources for your business at **OneYearRescuePlan.com**.

Made in the USA
Middletown, DE
26 April 2022